SPOT

COMMUNITY HELPERS

TEACHERS

by Golriz Golkar

amicus LEARNING

whiteboard

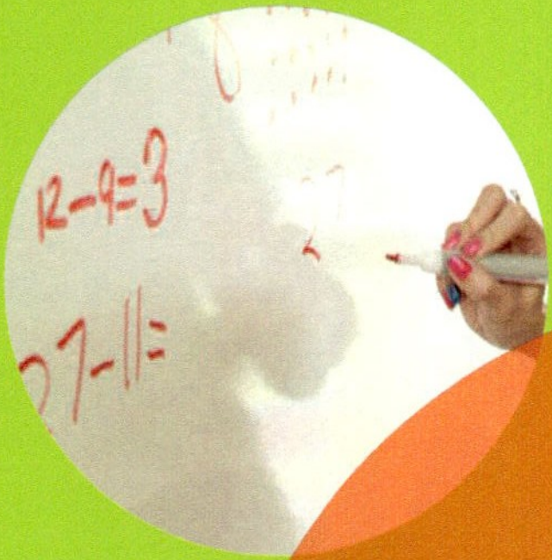

globe

Look for these words and pictures as you read.

book

ruler

Teachers help us.
What do they do?

The school bell rings.
It's time to learn!
The teacher writes
on the whiteboard.

whiteboard

globe

The teacher shows a globe.
Where is our city?
Oh! There we are!

It is story time!
The teacher picks a book.
She reads to the class.

book

ruler

The class plants seeds.
The teacher hands out rulers.
How tall did they grow?

It is time for art.
The teacher shows us what to do.

Teachers help us learn.
They teach us many things!